Library of Congress Cataloging-in-Publication Number 98-68462

ISBN 0-7624-0534-1

This book may be ordered by mail from the publisher.
Please include $2.50 for postage and handling.
But try your bookstore first!

Running Press Book Publishers
125 South Twenty-second Street
Philadelphia, Pennsylvania 19103-4399

Visit us on the web!
www.runningpress.com

If you are interested in ordering Bruce Blitz Video Kits, please visit your local
arts and crafts store, or send for a video kit catalog:
Blitz Art Products
P.O. Box 8022
Cherry Hill, NJ 08002
USA

THE *Blitz* FUN BOOK OF CARTOON PEOPLE

By Bruce Blitz

RUNNING PRESS
PHILADELPHIA · LONDON

CONTENTS

PART I
INSTRUCTION

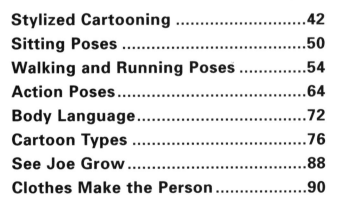

PART 2
ACTIVITIES

ABOUT THE AUTHOR

Bruce Blitz started out as the boy who drew funny pictures of the principal at school. Now he appears at numerous school assembly programs and demonstrates his cartooning skills to rave reviews from eveyone (including the principal!). He has been drawing professionally for more than twenty years.

Blitz is the creator and host of the internationally aired television series *Blitz on Cartooning*, which has earned four Emmy award nominations. He has authored several instructional books on drawing, produced a series of instructional drawing videos, and has appeared on a bunch of television programs, including *The Joan Rivers' Show*, Discovery Channel's *Start to Finish*, and the QVC Shopping Network. Blitz is mostly self-taught, thanks to his experience in a wide variety of artistic fields. He has operated his own animation company in Philadelphia and Las Vegas, where he produced cartoon television commercials and animated sequences.

An accomplished, professional musician performing on both piano and organ, Blitz wrote the music for his television show and all of his instructional videos. The music from *Blitz on Cartooning* was even nominated for an Emmy! He is also noted for his caricature work, having appeared nationwide at trade shows, conventions, vacation resorts, and the 1982 World's Fair in Knoxville, Tennessee.

He was born in Philadelphia, Pennsylvania, and now resides in Cherry Hill, New Jersey with his wife and two children.

HI AND WELCOME! I'M BRUCE BLITZ, AND I WAS JUST LOOKING OUT MY WINDOW AND NOTICING THE WIDE VARIETY OF PEOPLE WE HAVE IN THE WORLD. TALL, SHORT, HEAVY, THIN . . . THE LIST GOES ON AND ON. AND IN THIS FUN-FILLED CARTOONING BOOK, THAT'S WHAT WE'RE GOING TO EXPLORE . . . CARTOON PEOPLE! YOU CAN START WITH THE FRONT COVER. SEE HOW MANY COMBINATIONS YOU CAN MAKE, AND HOW MUCH FUN YOU CAN HAVE!

WHERE TO USE THIS BOOK

IN BED

ON A BUS

CARTOONS ARE EVERYWHERE

COMIC BOOKS

BUMPER STICKERS

CARTOON PORTRAITS

T-SHIRTS . . . A GREAT WAY TO ADVERTISE.

PRODUCT PACKAGING

CLIP ART FOR COMPUTER SOFTWARE

BUSINESS LOGOS

COMIC STRIPS IN THE NEWSPAPERS

ANIMATED
CARTOONS
ON TV

GRRRR-R

CARTOONS ARE
EVERYWHERE, AND IT'S
UP TO YOU AND ME TO
KEEP IT THAT WAY!

PART I

·INSTRUCTION·

NOW LET'S START LEARNING WHAT IT
TAKES TO DRAW CARTOON PEOPLE.

ART SUPPLIES

ALL YOU NEED
TO START DRAWING IS A
PENCIL, PAPER, AND AN IDEA.
THE SKY IS THE LIMIT!

PEN

A black marker with a medium point is a great place to start. By varying the hand pressure, you can get a thick or thin line—this versatility is essential for great cartooning.

PAPER

A pad of drawing paper—or even plain old copy-machine paper—works well.

LIGHT BOX

A light box allows you to see through two or three sheets of paper at a time. You can use it to make a clean drawing out of your "rough" cartoon.

A light box also allows you to reposition your original artwork to design a better composition, or just to improve on your first drawing.

ROUGH DRAWING

CLEANED-UP VERSION

MISCELLANEOUS ART SUPPLIES
These come in handy, too.

TRIANGLE AND RULER

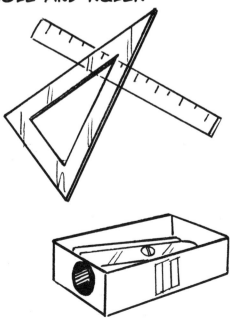

PENCIL SHARPENER

WHITE MASKING TAPE
(for covering mistakes and taping your drawings down)

TRACING PAPER

DRAWING CARTOON HEADS

First of all, let me show you how simple it is to draw a cartoon head.

1. Begin by drawing a shape (in this case, it's an oval) with two guidelines.

2. Using these guidelines, add eyes, eyebrows, and a nose.

3. Sketch in some ears and a mouth.

4. Add some hair and detail, and there's your finished cartoon head.

DIFFERENT SHAPES . . . DIFFERENT PEOPLE

DIAMOND SHAPE

TRIANGLE SHAPE

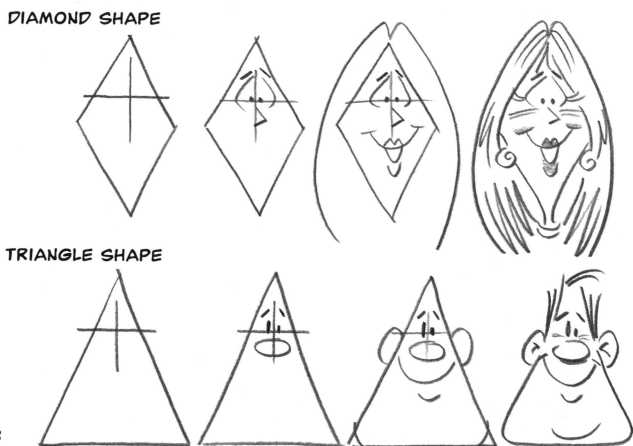

BEAN

UPSIDE-DOWN TEARDROP

A LONG OVAL

FREE FORM

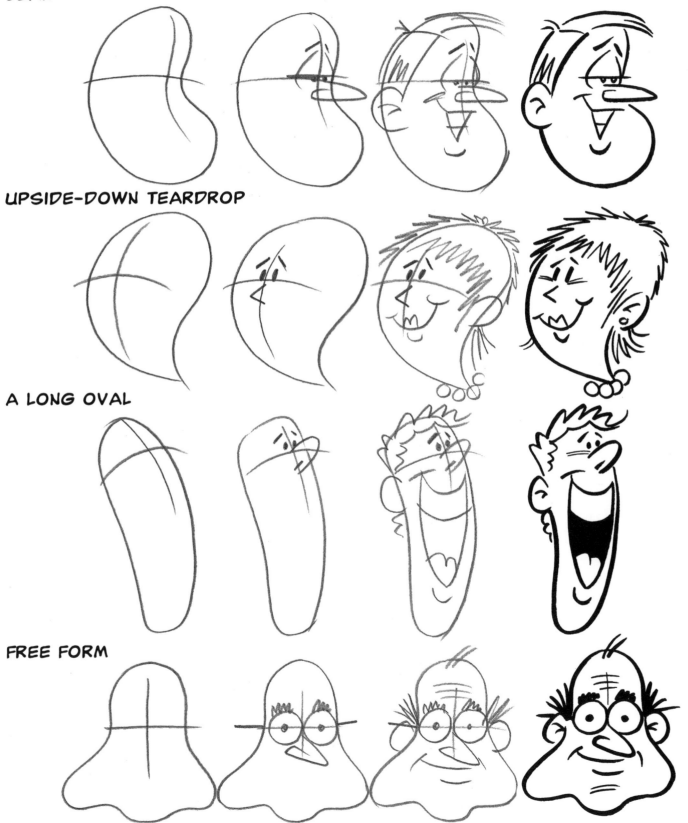

There are lots of shapes you can use to draw cartoon heads. Just look at all the great shapes there are in the supermarket, like Old Melonhead here.

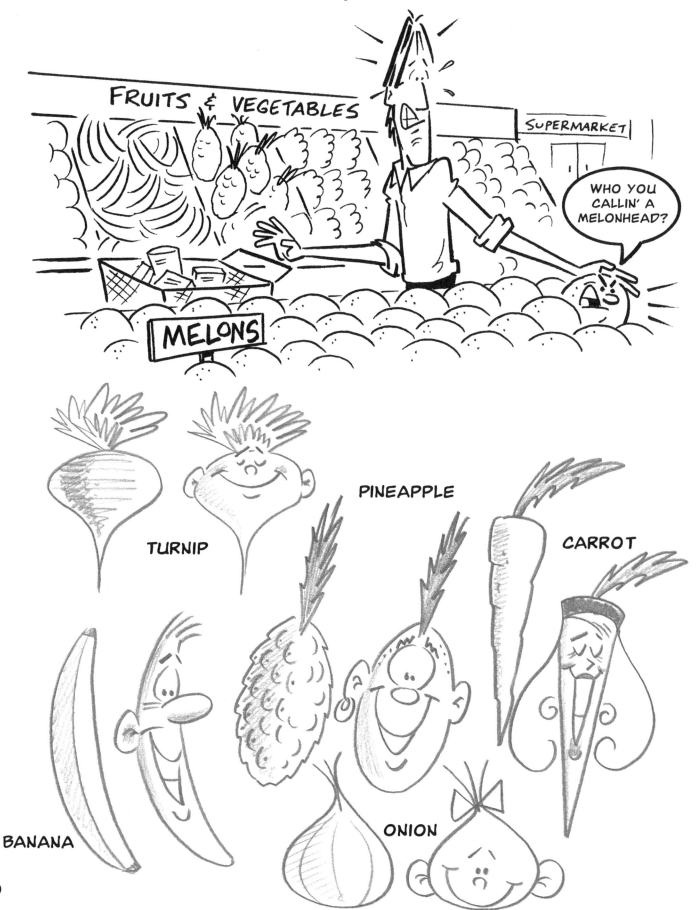

TURNIP

PINEAPPLE

CARROT

BANANA

ONION

TURNING HEADS

Think of the shape you begin with as a three-dimensional object—such as a balloon or an egg—and wrap the guidelines *around* the shape as I've done here. See! You can make your cartoons face in different directions!

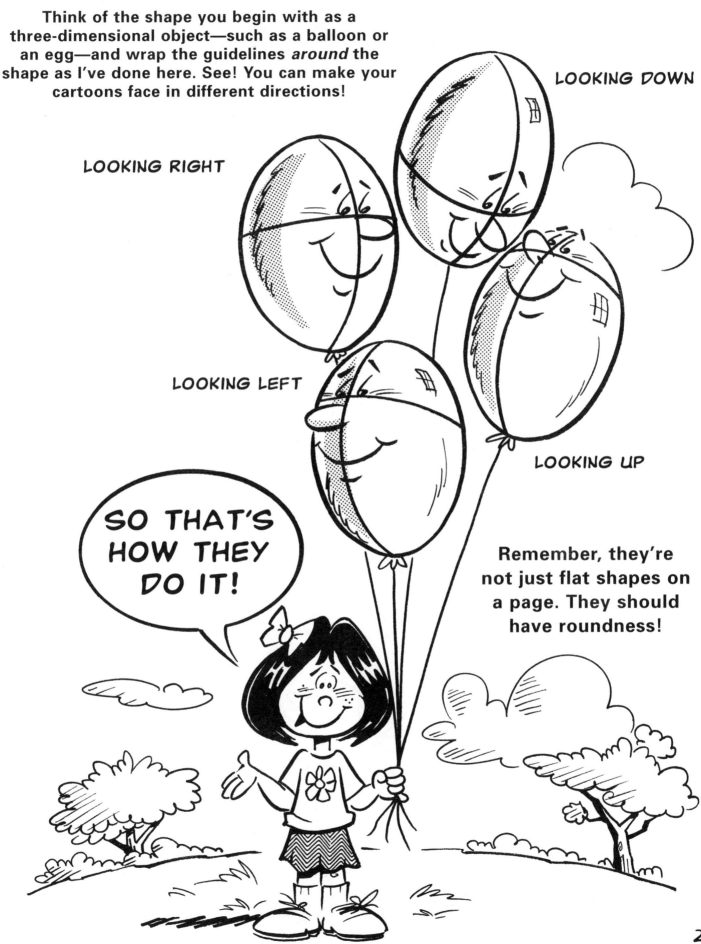

LOOKING DOWN

LOOKING RIGHT

LOOKING LEFT

LOOKING UP

SO THAT'S HOW THEY DO IT!

Remember, they're not just flat shapes on a page. They should have roundness!

FEATURES

You can't have a face without features, and it's the combination
of these features that gives your characters *character*.
The cartoon features below are simplified versions of the real thing.
See how many variations you can sketch on your own.

EYES

NOSES

MOUTHS

HAIR AND EARS

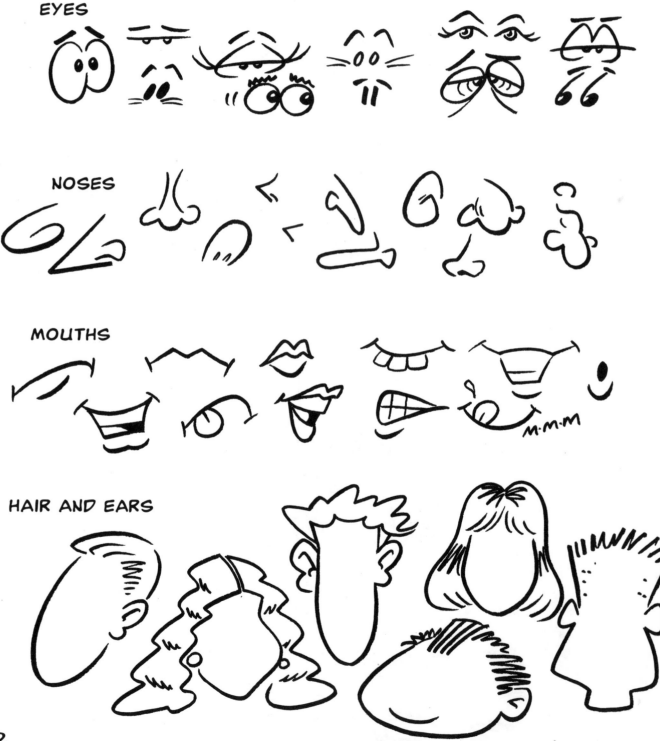

HOW TO "INK-IN" YOUR CARTOONS

Every cartoon you draw should start with pencil and end with ink.

STEP 1
Draw your cartoon in pencil. Don't worry about extra lines or stray marks. Make corrections as you go.

STEP 2
Once you are satisfied, go over the pencil line with your marker. Make one clean, definite line.

STEP 3
After the marker ink has dried, erase over the entire drawing. The pencil lines are gone, and the ink line stays!

STEP 4
There you have your finished, "inked-in," professional-looking cartoon.

EXPRESSIONS

Facial expressions are what breathe life into your cartoons. By mixing and matching the facial features, you can make your characters express different emotions. It's as if they can think!

WORRIED

UH OH! I JUST REMEMBERED SOMETHING.

Black lines drawn close together seem to create red cheeks.

One eyebrow up and one eyebrow down helps to create this expression.

HMMM ... I'M NOT TOO SURE ABOUT HIM!

SUSPICIOUS

CARTOON EFFECTS & ACCESSORIES

Do you notice all the extra little doodles around these drawings? I call these "cartoon effects and accessories." They add to the emotion or action in your drawings. You'll see more of these throughout the book.

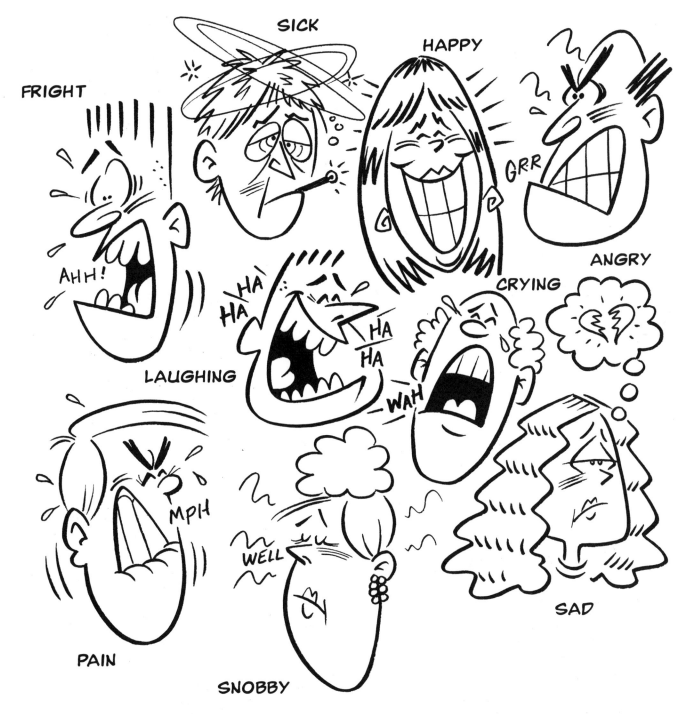

Practice making expressions in a mirror, and then drawing your face in cartoon-style lines. Add effects and accessories like teardrops, sweat drops, and dizzy lines, and words to express laughter, grunting noises, and anything else that works.

HANDS

The easiest method of creating good cartoon hands is to draw fingers on these next two shapes.

CIRCLE

 1.

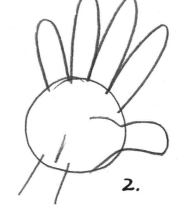 2.

 3.

SQUARE

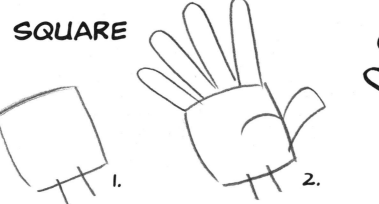 1. 2.

 3.

PRACTICE TIP

PRACTICE DRAWING HANDS BY USING YOUR OWN HANDS AS A MODEL.

BASIC HAND POSITIONS

Holding poses

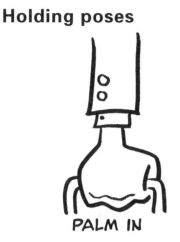

PALM IN

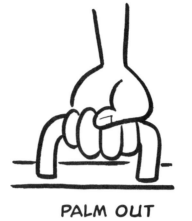

PALM OUT

SHAKE!

Hands can be . . .

CHOP

. . . **very expressive!**

FLiK

TWIDDLE

FEET

Feet are very important to the cartoon figure . . . not only
for the obvious reason of balance, but because they help to explain
the character's overall style and situation.

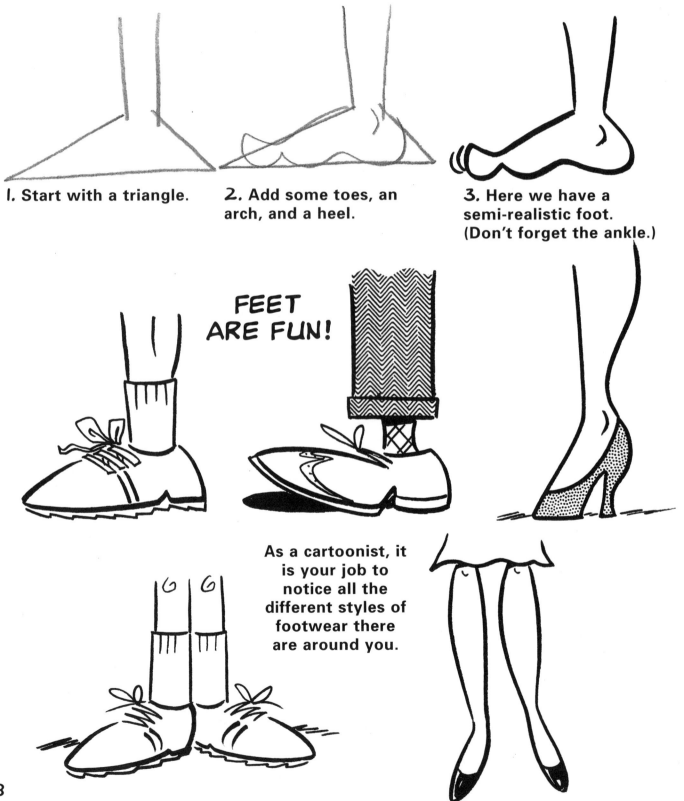

1. Start with a triangle.

2. Add some toes, an arch, and a heel.

3. Here we have a semi-realistic foot. (Don't forget the ankle.)

FEET ARE FUN!

As a cartoonist, it is your job to notice all the different styles of footwear there are around you.

Practice drawing feet in a variety of situations.

BLITZ TIPZ
NEVER GIVE UP! SUCCESS MAY ONLY BE INCHES AWAY.

CARTOON BODIES

Let's begin with the oldest method for drawing cartoon bodies: the stick figure.

See how easy it is to go from "stick" to "Rick."

RICK

l. Draw in a basic pose using the stick figure.

2. Add thickness to the lines. This is called "fleshing out."

3. Clean up your drawing and add detail to complete the sketch.

Notice how the hips and shoulders are at opposite angles in these two examples. This creates more of a "rhythm" to their poses.

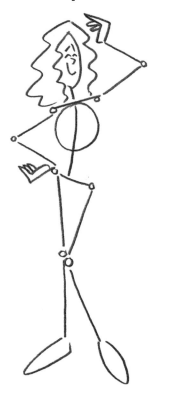

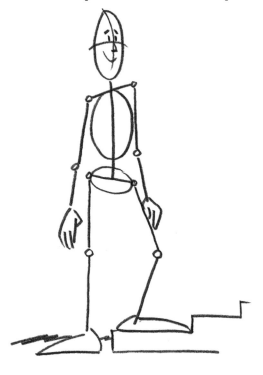

The stick figure should appear to be balanced, and not like it's ready to fall over.

Using stick figures helps you see the position instantly and clearly. Once you're satisfied with the pose, you can complete the drawing. On the next few pages, we will create some poses with the stick figure as our model. I added two ovals to the classic stick figure to help illustrate the pose.

TYPING

LIFTING

RECLINING

CLICK.

WALKING

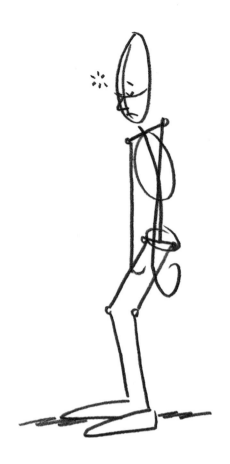

SLUMPING

SHAKING HANDS

GIVING A SPEECH

34

Practice by drawing lots of stick figures in as many positions as you can come up with!

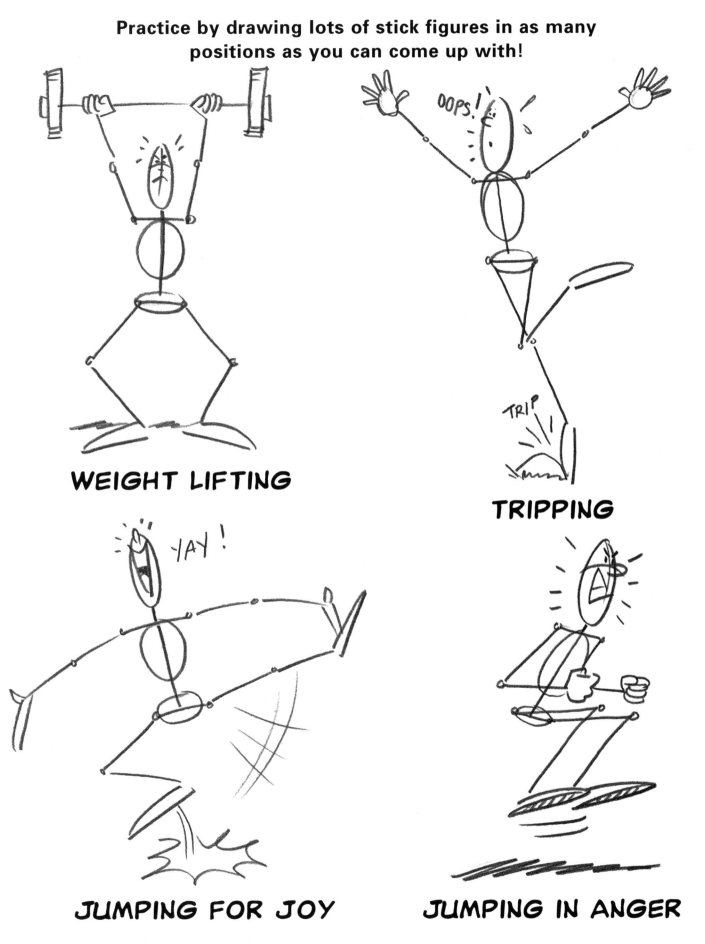

WEIGHT LIFTING

TRIPPING

JUMPING FOR JOY

JUMPING IN ANGER

FORM AND SHADING

It's important to learn the basic principles of form and shading. It's easy, and it will make your drawings appear to have a real, three-dimensional look. In other words, they will jump right off the page!

LIGHT SOURCE

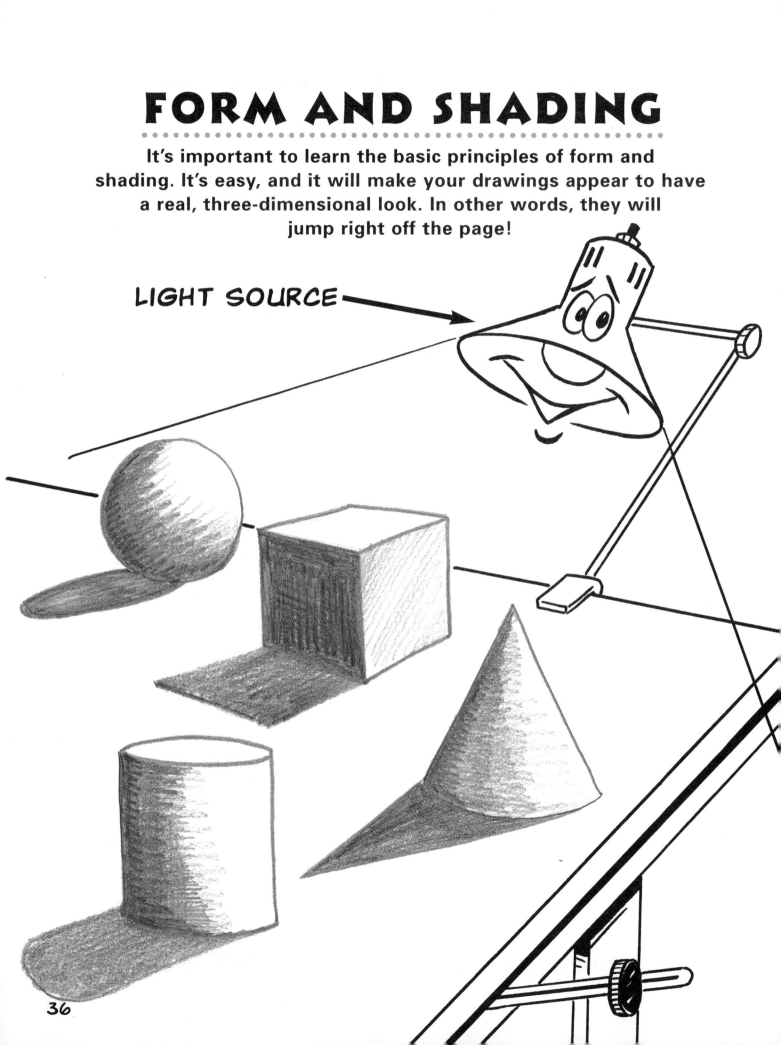

Here's How It's Done

SHAPE
Shape is two-dimensional; it has *length* and *width*.

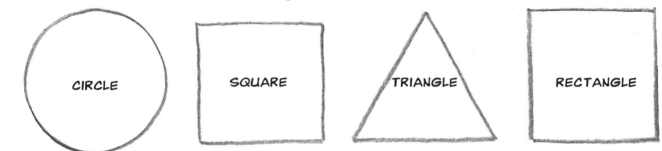

FORM
Now we have added a third dimension to the shape: depth.

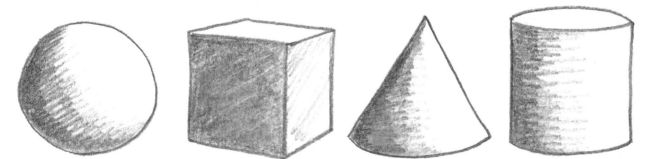

SHADING
Shading adds even more depth. It makes these forms appear to be *solid*. Decide which direction the light is coming from, then shade the opposite side. On rounded objects, the shading should become gradually lighter as it moves toward the light.

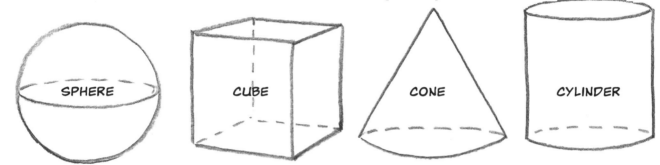

However, the shading changes abruptly where flat planes meet (as on the cube).

CAST SHADOW
Cast shadow extends from the shaded side of the object and takes on the shape of the object itself. This completes the illusion of depth.

LET'S APPLY THE PRINCIPLES OF FORM AND SHADING TO THE HUMAN FIGURE.

You will find that the parts of the body break down to these basic forms, though the resemblance may not be exact. For example, the head is not quite round, but it does resemble a sphere.

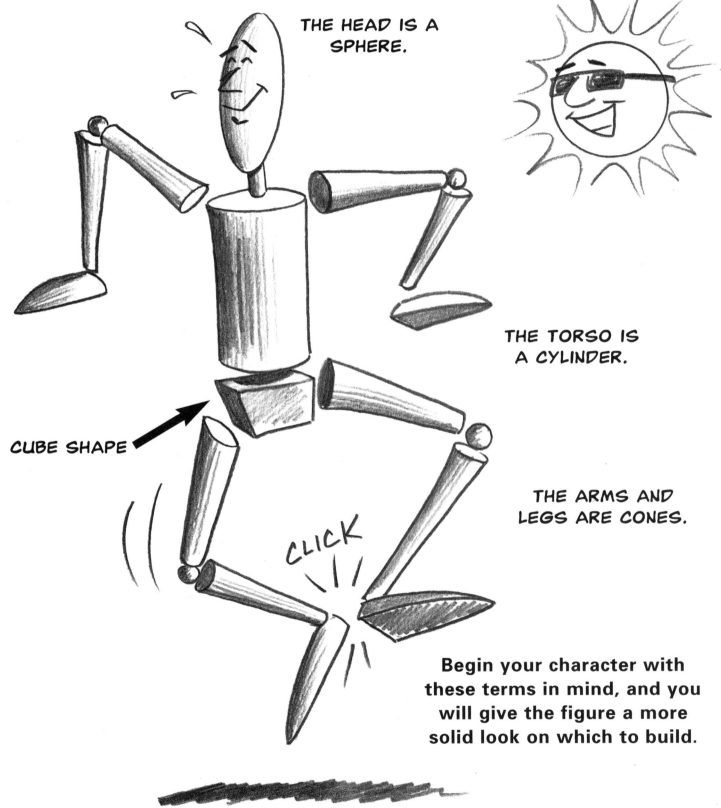

THE HEAD IS A SPHERE.

THE TORSO IS A CYLINDER.

CUBE SHAPE

THE ARMS AND LEGS ARE CONES.

CLICK

Begin your character with these terms in mind, and you will give the figure a more solid look on which to build.

Remember, the first question to ask yourself when applying shading and cast shadow is: *From which direction is the light coming?*

WHERE IS THE LIGHT SOURCE IN THIS DRAWING?

CORRECT! THE LEFT SIDE.

You're doing fine. Check out the next couple of pages for more Form & Shading.

On these two pages, draw an arrow in the direction
from which the light is coming.

STYLIZED CARTOONING

Now let's try cartooning the human figure in a completely different way. These figures will be built up from various shapes to create a more "stylized, flat" look.

SIDE VIEW

I. A triangle is a terrific shape from which to create many characters.

2. Add a head.

3. Add legs and shoes.

4. Draw in the rest of the details: face, hands, bow tie, and lapel.

5. Once you're satisfied with your sketch, use your marker to draw over the pencil with one clean, definite line.

6. After the ink dries, erase the pencil and there is your finished cartoon!

FRONT VIEW

This same shape can be used to draw a little girl.

TRIANGLE VARIATIONS

These triangles have been turned on their sides. The flat side is going up and down rather than across the bottom (like with the previous examples).

The flat side is the back of this character.

The flat side is the front of this guy.

SQUARES AND RECTANGLES

OVALS COME IN A WIDE VARIETY

WIDE

FIGURE 8

NARROW

VARIATIONS ON COMMON SHAPES

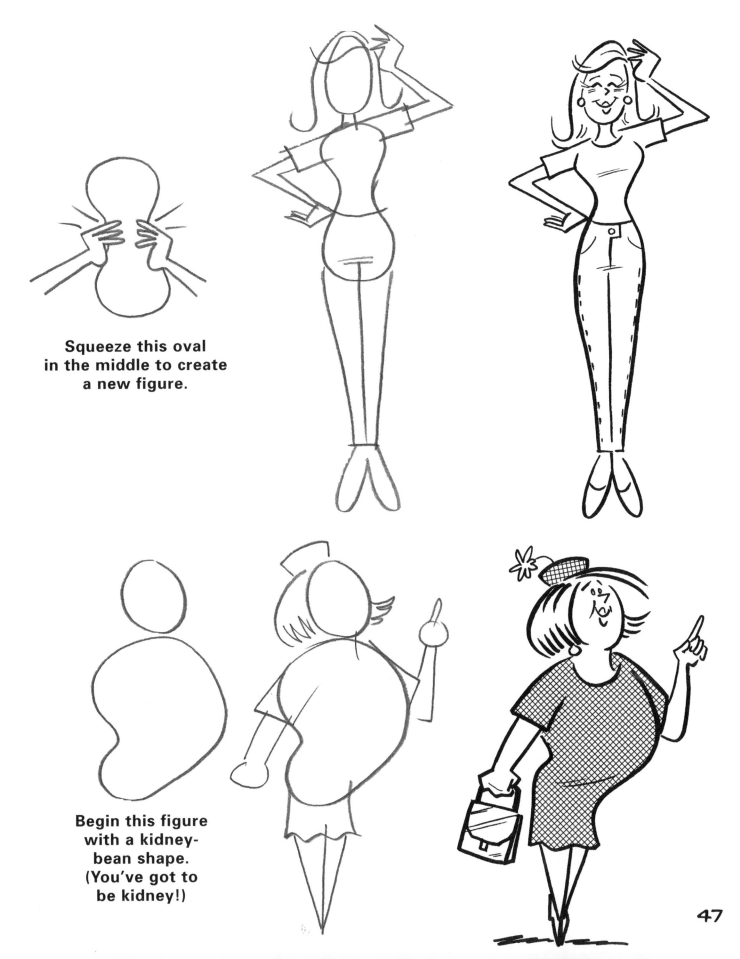

Squeeze this oval in the middle to create a new figure.

Begin this figure with a kidney-bean shape. (You've got to be kidney!)

MORE VARIATIONS ON COMMON SHAPES

This curved triangle is a great shape to use to create a lifeguard.

LIFEGUARD

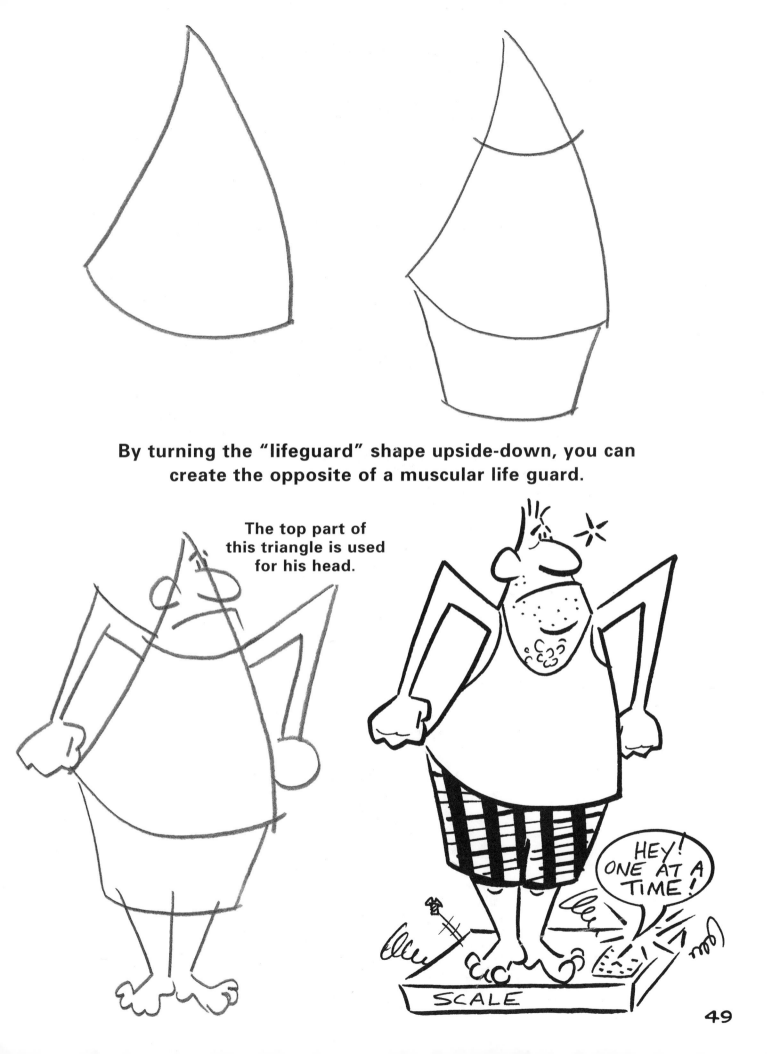

By turning the "lifeguard" shape upside-down, you can create the opposite of a muscular life guard.

The top part of this triangle is used for his head.

HEY! ONE AT A TIME!

SCALE

49

50

Cartoonists find that sitting poses come in very handy (or "footy," since they take the chartacters off their feet!).

Here is a side-view of a figure sitting. Notice how he is leaning forward and how his feet are arranged. This is a good example of "body language."
(More about that on page 72.)

FRONT-VIEW SITTING

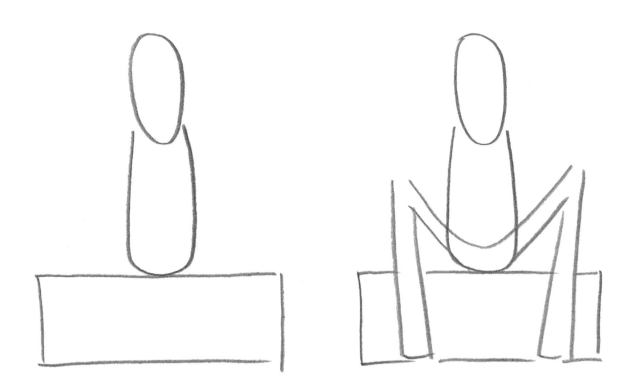

Simple first stages . . .
. . . are built into great cartoons.

PRACTICE!

SIDE-VIEW SITTING

1.

2.

3.

3/4-VIEW SITTING

This stick figure is a good start for a typical walking character. He is leaning back, taking long strides, and smiling. This is a confident walking pose.

l. Begin with our "new" friend, the stick figure.

2. Flesh it out . . .

3. . . . And he's on his way!

55

SIDE-VIEW WALK

1. Begin with the number eight.

2. Add triangles for legs.

3. Add some details . . .

4. . . . And there you have it—a busy executive walking to an important meeting!

3/4-VIEW WALK

Start with a hot dog shape.

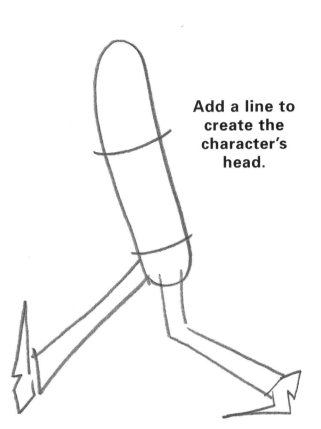

Add a line to create the character's head.

Fill in features.

HE LOOKS PRETTY DETERMINED. HIS TIE FLAPPING OVER HIS SHOULDER ADDS A LIVELY TOUCH.

Add effects and complete the drawing.

3/4-VIEW WALK

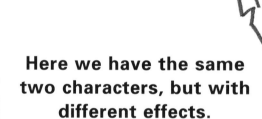

Here we have the same two characters, but with different effects.

By having the shadow meet his feet, he appears to be walking casually.

But by changing his facial expression to "worried," leaving a gap between his heel and shadow, and adding a few effects and accessories, he appears to be trotting as if he were in a hurry!

FRONT-VIEW WALK

Notice how the front leg appears to be larger than the back leg. This is called *perspective*. When you have two objects that are the same size, the one that is closer to you will appear larger.

COMIC WALK

Making the character bend down with his leg stretched forward creates a funny cartoon walk!

LET'S HAVE SOME "RUN FUN!"

SIDE VIEW

The "line of motion" here illustrates his body bent forward.

Adding cartoon effects & accessories really shows the reader what this character is doing.

SCARED RUN

The "line of motion" here is bent backwards, which is opposite of the running pose on the last page.

With both arms stretched forward and an expression of fright, this guy is obviously running from something.

A JOGGER

All elements here suggest
a leisurely run, especially
the expression on her face.

FRONT VIEW

The fist on the left appears larger than the one on the right because it is positioned closer to the reader's eye. This is another good example of *perspective*.

3/4 VIEW

Sports cartoons are a great place to begin for action! As with running poses, it's important to see the *line of motion*.

TENNIS PLAYER

**Line of
Motion**

SKI JUMPER

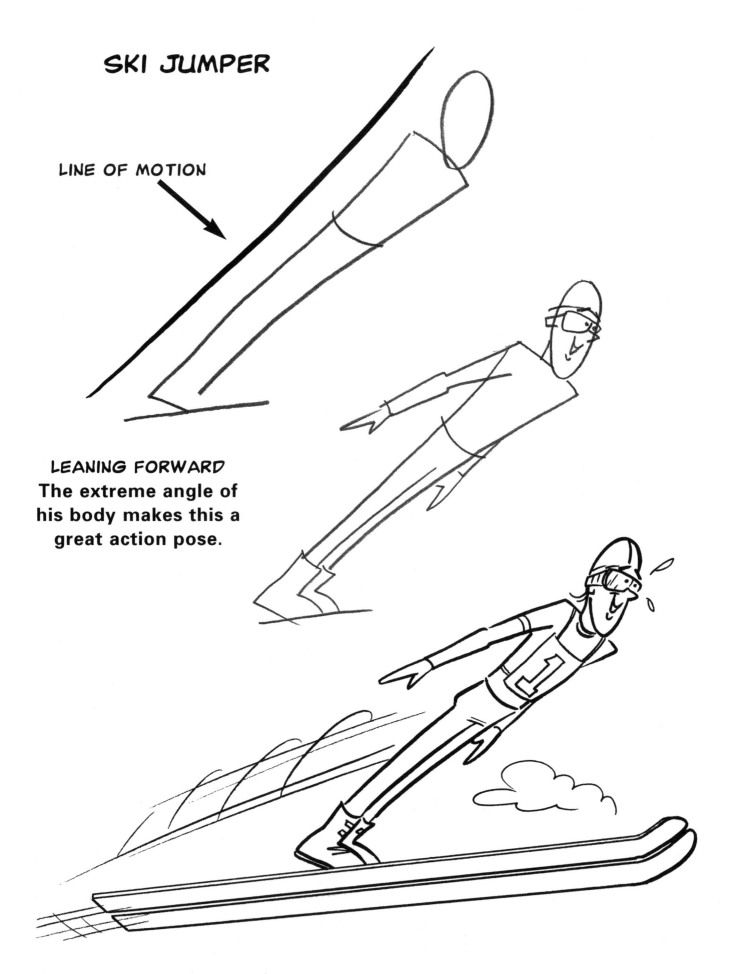

LINE OF MOTION

LEANING FORWARD
The extreme angle of his body makes this a great action pose.

BASKETBALL PLAYER

1. Begin with three shapes.

2. Add some lines for limbs and shapes for feet.

3. Add some more detail . . .

4. . . . And she's ready to make her move!

Who would have believed it? This same basic stick figure can be used to draw these two completely different characters.

BALLERINA

FOOTBALL PLAYER

SURFER

LUMBERJACK

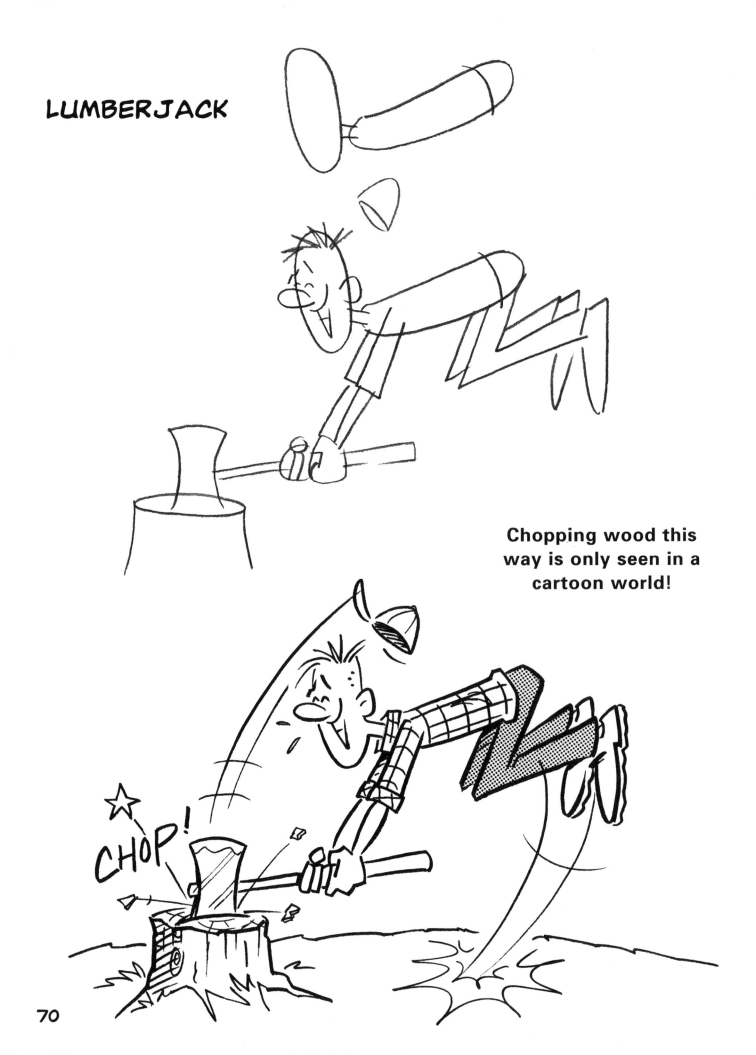

Chopping wood this
way is only seen in a
cartoon world!

CHOP!

ROLLERBLADER
(DON'T TRY THIS AT HOME!)

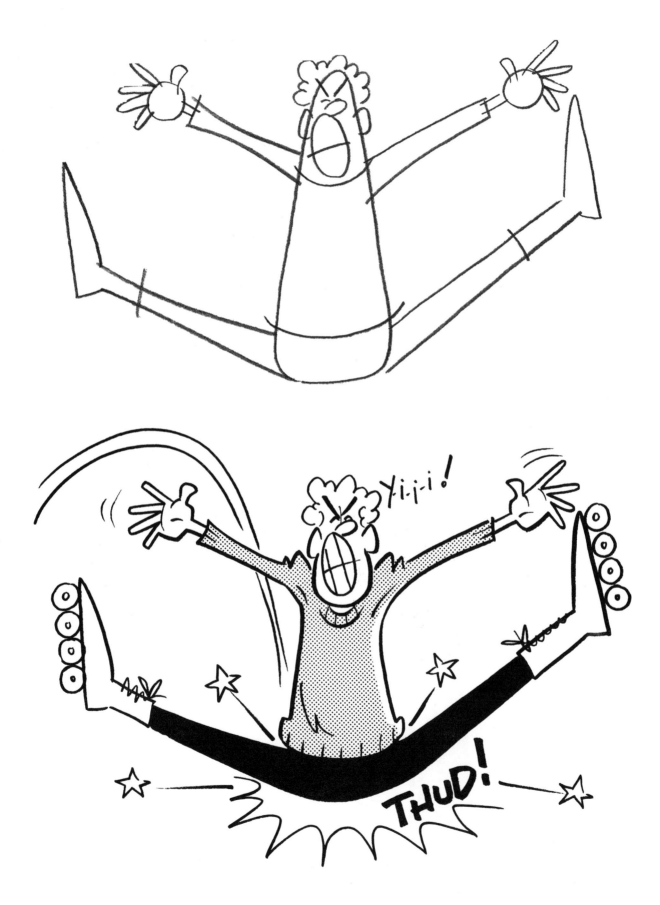

BODY LANGUAGE

When the facial expression is accompanied by an expressive body pose, you create "body language." This really lets your reader know what your character is thinking and feeling.

ANGRY

• The lines around his head show that he is "steaming" mad
• Arms folded
• Body leaning forward
• Foot tapping

TAP
TAP
TAP

HAPPY
He looks like he just got some good news.
In fact, he's jumping for joy!

PROUD
Her hand is on her hip and she
is standing straight and tall.
The lines around her head
indicate that she is glowing.

THINKING

He is looking for the answer by leaning forward and rubbing his chin. Also, note his knitted eyebrows.

SAD

He looks like the loneliest guy on the street because of the way he is sitting.

SCARED

She just heard a noise. Where is it coming from?

Her arms and legs are bent in an awkward manner, showing fear.

BLITZ TIPZ

WEEEEE!

BUDDING CARTOONIST

HARD WORK

SUCCESS

Working hard at something you enjoy should be fun.

CARTOON TYPES

People come in all shapes, sizes, and colors. Just look around you on your daily travels; you're bound to see plenty of people who fit into specific categories. How many "types" can you think of?

BASKETBALL PLAYER

MODEL

SPACEMAN

As the cartoonist, it's your job to find the right types
to play the parts in your cartoon world.

"NOT SO NICE" GUYS

Bullies and bad guys are important characters for every cartoonist. Here are two effective types of bad guys. . . .

BIG, MEAN BULLY

THIN, SLEAZY CROOK

Notice how both are drawn to look like they need a shave.

78

But wait . . . here comes the "Hero Type" to the rescue!

THE HERO TYPE SHOULD HAVE:
- Muscles
- Lots of hair
- A confident expression
- A strong chin
- Tights (optional!)

Note: See how learning running poses has already come in handy?! (Especially for these two guys.)

ALIENS

When it comes to creating aliens, nobody knows what is right or wrong. So have fun with it, and let your imagination go out of this world!

BEEP   BEEP

IS FOR ALIEN

IS FOR SPACESHIP

These are called "Doodle Tricks." You'll find many more of these in Part 2 of this book.

HI EARTH

INTELLIGENT TYPES

Bookworms and computer whizzes are interesting characters that share many common details.

- Neat hair
- Large glasses
- Well-groomed
- Books and computers as nearby props

BABIES
Babies are fun to draw and are always very dramatic. There are certain rules to keep in mind when drawing babies.

The head is almost 2/3 of the entire figure.

NOTICE THERE IS NO CHIN, AND HIS MOUTH LINE IS AT THE BOTTOM OF HIS HEAD.

I'M STANDING . . . . NOW WHAT?

His body can be constructed from a teardrop.

He's finally asleep . . . so let's move quietly to the next page.

Z-Z-Z-Z-Z

JUST KIDDING AROUND
Kids are always very active.

AGES 4 TO 7
She is approximately three-heads tall (and loves to paint).

3 YEARS
12 YEARS

Lowering the chin line adds years to a character.

THIS GUY COULD PASS FOR AGES 7 TO 9.

DIVING
(He better turn his body soon, or he's in for a major bellyflop.)

SPROING

TEENS

Teens have bodies almost as tall as adults, but they are skinnier and their faces look younger.

PLAYING A TRUMPET

LISTENING TO MUSIC

You can draw teens in a wide variety of interesting poses.

SENIOR CITIZENS
This type can be used for many comic situations.

TAKE THIS HAPPY OLD GUY DRINKING
HIS YOUTH TONIC. . . .

BALD HEAD WITH A
FEW LOOSE HAIRS

FEW TEETH

BONY LIMBS

Another way to draw older people is to give them a rounder, less comical appearance—as in these two examples . . .

Old people have a lot of free time, and so they participate in many interesting hobbies. Try to notice what old people do and make cartoons out of them!

GARDENING

KNITTING

SEE JOE GROW

These two pages were fun to draw! Try an age progression of your own. First create a character and redraw that character at various stages of his or her life. Study the character on these pages to find the differences that mark his various stages of growth. It's a great exercise!

6 MONTHS
Just a baby so far.

3 YEARS
Walking, talking, and playing with toys.

9 YEARS
Joe has found sports, but lost his teeth.

14 YEARS
Now he is in junior high school, and doing quite well.

25 YEARS
His first real job,
and he's ready to
shake hands with
a bright future.

50 YEARS
Not quite retired
yet, but he spends
more and more time
golfing these days.

75 YEARS
Joe still gets around
pretty well, and he
likes to keep up with
the news.

CLOTHES MAKE THE PERSON

Clothes are an important element and add great variety to your characters. Sometimes, clothes can be the most important aspect of your character.

PIRATE
- Vest
- Eye patch
- Belt buckle
- Sword
- Boots
- Facial hair

CONSTRUCTION WORKER
- Hard hat
- Work clothes
- Lunch pail
- Wrench

COLONIAL WOMAN

Look through history books for ideas.

SCRATCH SCRATCH

CAVE MAN

Not much clothing here, but enough to establish who he is and where he comes from. (The question is, how is the leopard dressed now?)

SHEIK
- Headdress
- Beard
- Robe

SUNBATHER
- Baseball hat
- Sunglasses
- Camera
- Swim trunks
- Towel
- Suntan lotion
- Sandals

SUN TAN OIL

HULA DANCER
- Flower in hair
- Lei around neck
- Grass skirt
- Bare feet

COWBOY
- Hat
- Sheriff's star
- Guns
- Boots and spurs

93

PART 2

·ACTIVITIES·

DOODLE TRICKS

Learn to turn numbers, letters, and
words into finished cartoons!

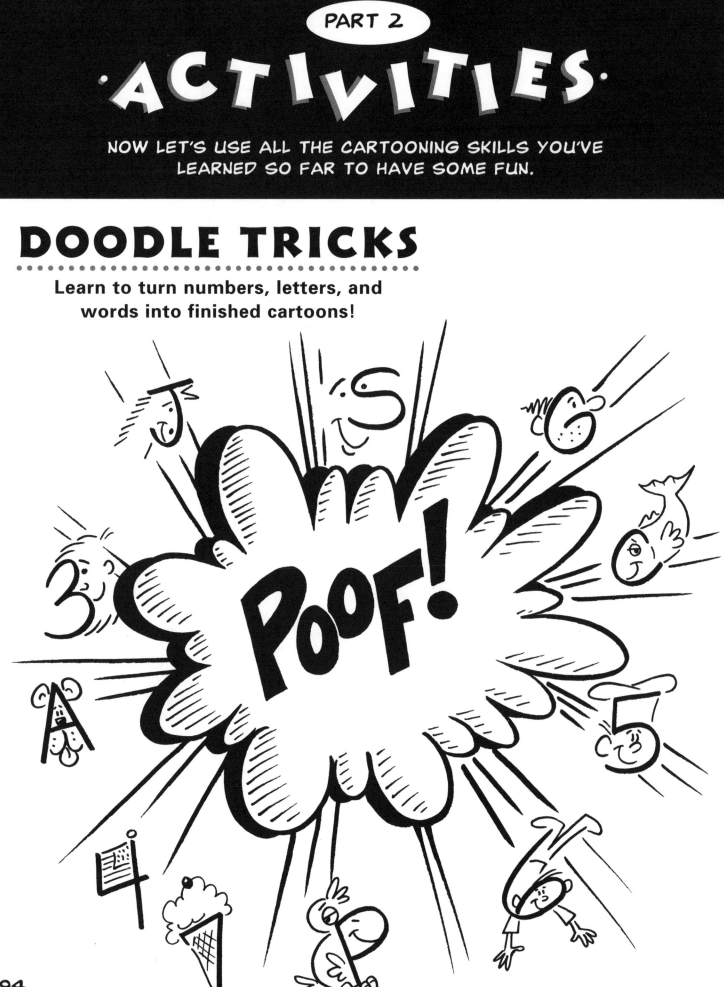

NUMBERTOONS

There are many possibilities for turning every
number into a cool cartoon. This exercise is fun and helps
to develop your cartooning skills.

NUMBER COMBOTOONS

Can you find all the numbers in these cartoons?

ACTIVITY
On a clean sheet of paper, write down the numbers 1 through 10. Make sure they
are as big as the numbers above. Then, create your very own numbertoons!

ALPHABETTOONS
People love to see a cartoonist turn letters into finished sketches.

The finished alphabettoons don't have to have anything to do with the letter that you use to create them.

PRACTICE LIKE ME . . . FROM A TO "Z."

ACTIVITY
On a clean sheet of paper, write down the letters of the alphabet. Make sure they are as big as the letters above. Then, create your very own alphabettoons!

WORDTOONS
**These wordtoons demonstrate how the end result
can illustrate the word itself.**

hop

Dog

Bug

**Notice how most of the drawing is completed simply
by writing the letter, word, or number.**

TALK

NAMETOONS

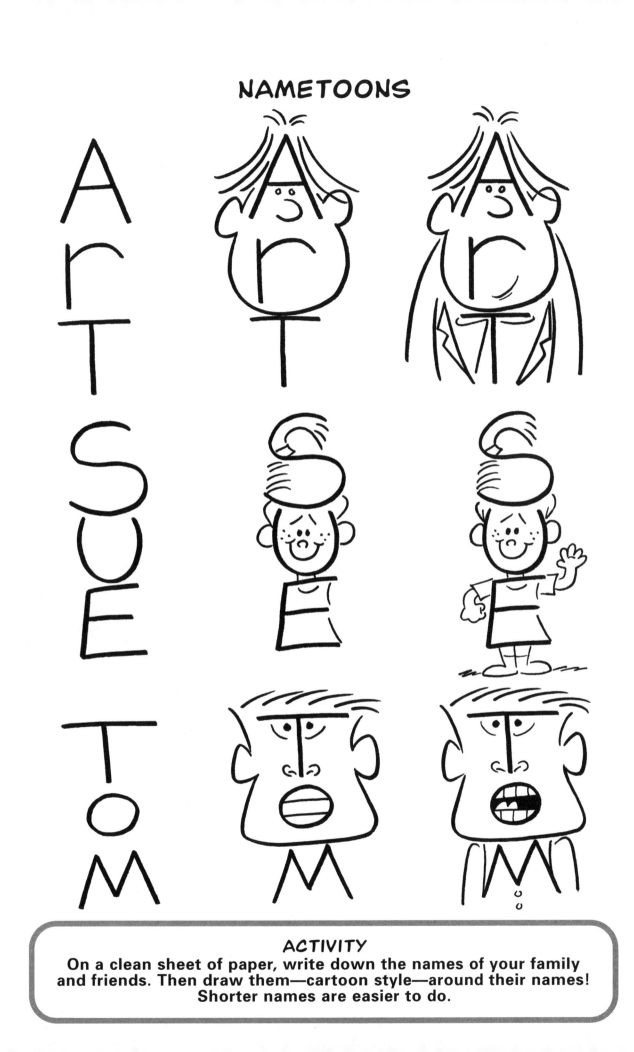

ACTIVITY
On a clean sheet of paper, write down the names of your family
and friends. Then draw them—cartoon style—around their names!
Shorter names are easier to do.

CHALK TALK

CHALK TALK IS GREAT ENTERTAINMENT! YOU GET TO DRAW CARTOONS FOR AN AUDIENCE, AND THEY ALWAYS LOVE IT. WHEN YOU PERFORM CHALK TALK, YOU SHOULD ALWAYS USE A LARGE PAD OF PAPER, AN EASEL, THICK MARKERS, AND A LOT OF PERSONALITY! REMEMBER TO SMILE A LOT, TELL SOME JOKES, AND ASK YOUR AUDIENCE TO PARTICIPATE. YOU CAN PERFORM CHALK TALK FOR YOUR FRIENDS, AT SCHOOL, OR AT FAMILY PARTIES. IT'S ALWAYS A HIT! A GOOD CHALK TALK PERFORMANCE USUALLY TELLS A STORY OR GAG THAT FEATURES AN UNEXPECTED ENDING. TAKE THIS SKETCH OF A FROG, FOR EXAMPLE. IF YOU TURN THIS PAGE UPSIDE DOWN, YOU WILL SEE HIM TURN INTO SOMETHING ELSE. . . .

SEEING EYE TO EYE

Here are some things you may want to say in your presentation. Remember, these are just guidelines. You can say anything, as long as you tell the story.

1. Once there was a man who had his eyes examined, only to find he had perfect 20/20 vision.

2. But after further examination, it turned out . . .

3. . . . this guy had a different kind of "I" trouble.

CHUBTOONS

Weight *until you see the cartoons on these next two pages . . .*
pretty heavy stuff!

He was a lot thinner . . .
. . . before he ate his dinner.

Just add the extra line!

. . . And some cartoon effects!

Pigs have curly tails like this. With a few added features we get the whole pig.

(DON'T FORGET HIS CURLY TAIL)

THE ELEPHANT

Here's a good trick that will surprise everyone. First, show your audience the cartoon with the two guys (below).

1. Let's see if we can figure out this guy's riddle by drawing an elephant.

2. Add the eyes and trunk.

3. Add two ears and a mouth, and there he is. Now, why can't you get *down* from an elephant?

YOU CAN'T GET *DOWN* FROM AN ELEPHANT!

WHY NOT?

Turn this sketch over for the answer.

Answer: Because you get *down* from a duck.

A CARTOONIST AND HIS LAMP

HOW TO PREPARE
"A CARTOONIST AND HIS LAMP."

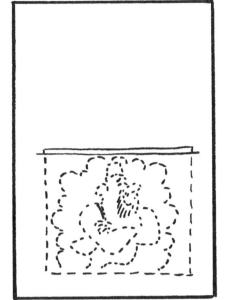

FRONT VIEW OF THE PAGE YOU'LL BE DRAWING THE LAMP ON.

l. Cut a horizontal slit in the paper you will be drawing on.

2. On a separate piece of paper, draw a genie and place it behind the page with about 1/4 inch of the genie sketch peeking up through the slit. (This shouldn't be visible to the audience.)

3. Pull the genie up for a great surprise ending.

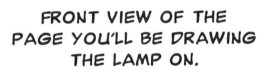

BACK VIEW OF THE PAGE.

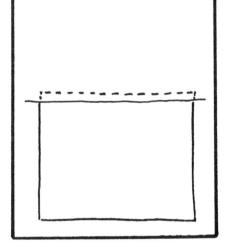

PREPARED DRAWING OF THE GENIE.

IF HE GRANTS YOU ANY WISHES, IT WILL BE AN EVEN BIGGER SURPRISE TO ME.

THE AUTOMATIC BANK TELLER
(OR . . . "TELLER YOURSELF")

1. Turn to a new page in your pad and say . . .

I'M NOW GOING TO SKETCH ONE OF THOSE AUTOMATIC BANK TELLERS!

2. Your drawing should look something like this. You won't need too much detail. Then you say . . .

HOW DOES A CARTOONIST GET MONEY? HE WITHDRAWS IT!!

HOW TO PREPARE
"THE AUTOMATIC BANK TELLER"

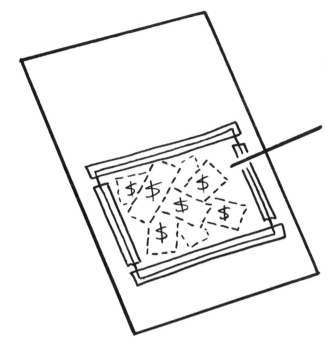

1. Get some play money (or use real money) and place it behind the sheet of paper that the audience will see. Tape another piece of paper completely over all the money to keep it in place.

2. During your presentation, say, "Oops! . . . I forgot to draw a slot for my card!" and draw a slot over the place where you have already secretly cut one. Then insert your card and say, "Ah . . . now it should work!"

3. Before beginning the gag, cut a slit in the front of the paper. Then, after you have drawn the automatic bank teller for the audience, simply lift along the "get money" line and watch it all come tumbling out!

CARTOON FLIP BOOK

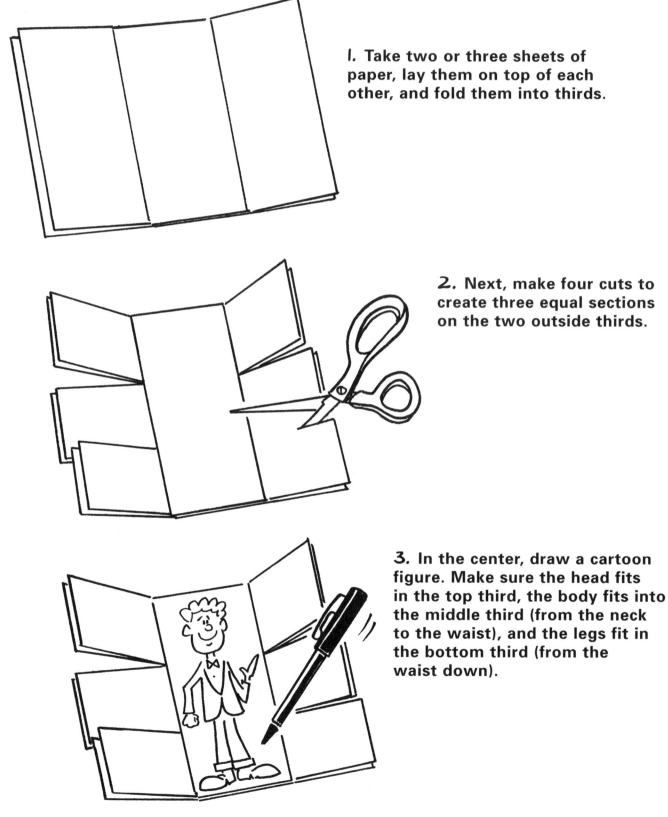

1. Take two or three sheets of paper, lay them on top of each other, and fold them into thirds.

2. Next, make four cuts to create three equal sections on the two outside thirds.

3. In the center, draw a cartoon figure. Make sure the head fits in the top third, the body fits into the middle third (from the neck to the waist), and the legs fit in the bottom third (from the waist down).

4. Flip over one panel at a time and draw different heads, bodies, and legs. By mixing the pages up, you'll create tons of wacky cartoon combinations. The more pieces of paper you begin with in Step 1, the more combinations you'll get.

Here are just some of the possibilities. . . .

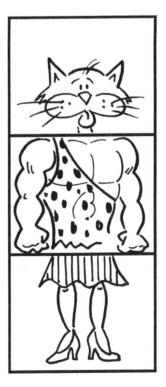

LONGTOOOOOONS

Here is a neat visual effect.

1. Draw your cartoons as if they got stretched out.

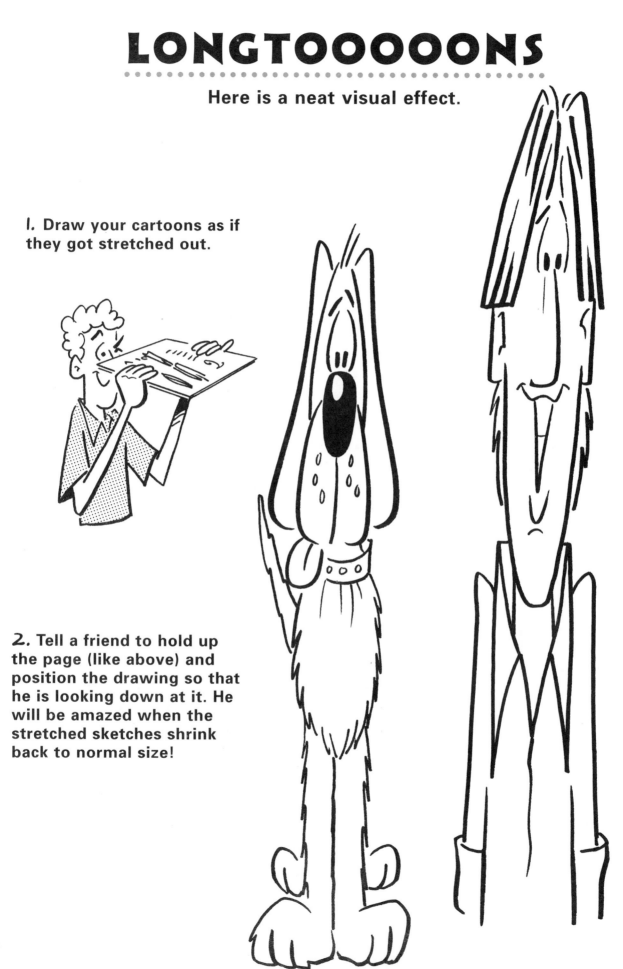

2. Tell a friend to hold up the page (like above) and position the drawing so that he is looking down at it. He will be amazed when the stretched sketches shrink back to normal size!

FOLD-A-TOON

All you need for this game are three people willing to laugh and have fun.

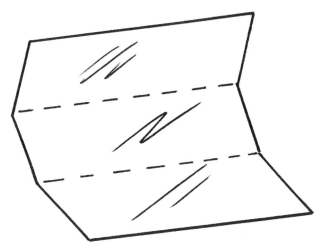

I. Fold a piece of paper into thirds.

2. Have the first person draw a cartoon head (person, animal, whatever) on the top third. Make sure the *neck lines* run just over the fold line, then fold the section back so that no one can see the head.

3. The next person, starting with the *neck lines*, draws a body and arms. Make sure the outside *body lines* run just over the fold line, then fold the section back so no one can see the body or the head.

4. Starting with the *body lines*, the third person draws the legs and feet.

5. Open the paper up to see the masterpiece!

113

MAKE PAUL TALL
(OR STRETCH THE SKETCH)

1. Draw a cartoon person and cut a slit just below the waist (see dotted line).

2. On a second sheet of paper, draw a long pair of legs that will fit into the slit you cut in Step 1. Cut the legs out right up to the black outline and insert them through the slit.

3. By sliding these legs up and down you can make Paul tall (or short).

PUNTOONS

Drawing cartoons to illustrate words that have more than one meaning can be very punny!

Here are some examples.

FEELING TENTS

HAVE A NICE DAY!

CABIN FEVER

PIER PRESSURE

Start by making a list of words that are pronounced the same but mean different things. (These are called *homonyms*—for example, "tents" and "tense"; or "peer" and "pier.") Next, think of a familiar phrase that uses that word, and illustrate it.

LOOKING PAIL

THE "DAFFY"-NITION OF PHOTOGRAPHER:

A PITCHER TAKER

BLITZ TIPZ

Well Done . . . is better than . . . Well Said!

Don't talk about doing something . . . just do it!

MAKE MOE THROW!

This next project is a great way to add movement to your drawings! Photocopy or trace the cartoon at the bottom of the next page. Do the same for the wheel of balls at the top of the next page. On your copy, cut along the dotted lines in each picture.

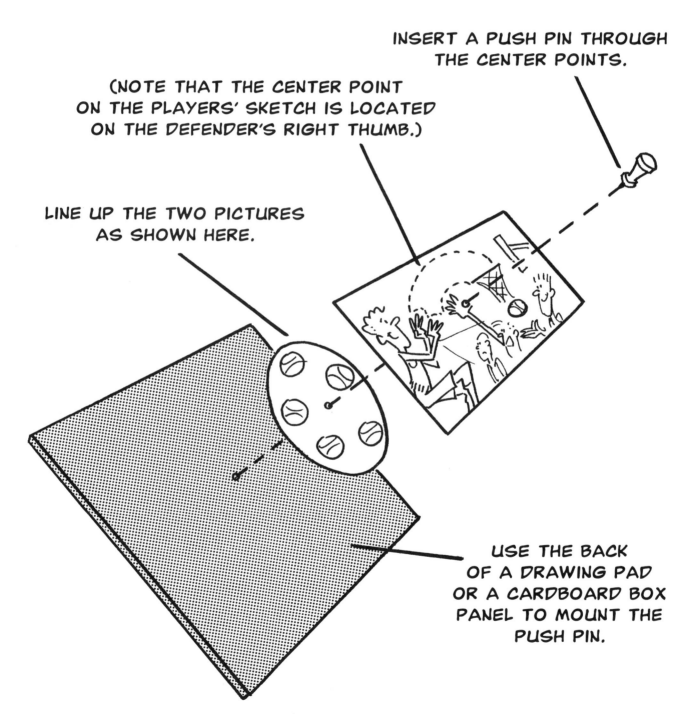

INSERT A PUSH PIN THROUGH THE CENTER POINTS.

(NOTE THAT THE CENTER POINT ON THE PLAYERS' SKETCH IS LOCATED ON THE DEFENDER'S RIGHT THUMB.)

LINE UP THE TWO PICTURES AS SHOWN HERE.

USE THE BACK OF A DRAWING PAD OR A CARDBOARD BOX PANEL TO MOUNT THE PUSH PIN.

Turn the wheel to score! Hey . . . this guy never misses!

FLIP-BOOK ANIMATION

The flipbook is one of the oldest methods that artists use to make drawings move. Here is a simple project to help you learn about how *animation* works.

YOU'LL NEED AN EMPTY SKETCH PAD OR A NOTEBOOK

A PENCIL OR PEN

TITLE: THE RUNNING DOG. (PRETTY SNAPPY HUH?)

Use these two drawings to create the illusion of a running dog. Photocopy or trace these two drawings, making sure to include the "cross hairs" or registration marks—these ensure that the drawings will be in the correct position for smooth animation.

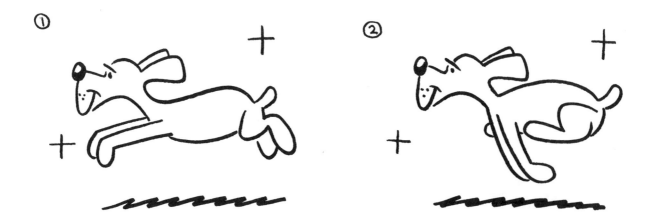

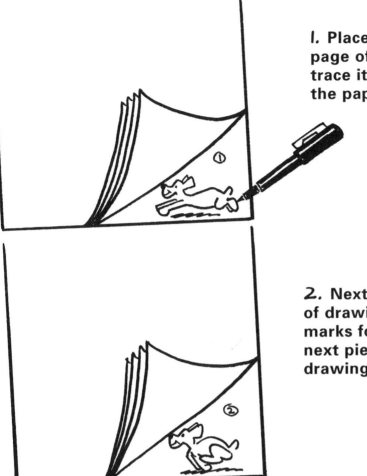

1. Place drawing 1 under the last page of your drawing pad, and trace it. If you can't see through the paper, refer to page 16.

2. Next, place drawing 2 on top of drawing 1 (use the registration marks for this). Pull down the next piece of paper and trace drawing 2 on it.

3. Repeat steps 1 and 2 over the last thirty pages of your pad (or more!). Then, flip the pages from the back of the pad to the front, and see the dog run! You can create your own sequences!

FIND THE DIFFERENCES

Can you find ten differences in these two drawings?

RIDE 'EM!

Make a photocopy of this page.

Can you make this guy ride?

It can be done!
Answer on page 126

ON YOUR COPY, CUT ALONG THE DOTTED LINE.

CREATE YOUR OWN "FIND THE DIFFERENCES" PUZZLE. HERE'S HOW:

Draw a busy scene, and leave out several elements here and there.
Next, photocopy your drawing and draw in the missing elements. Make the differences as easy or difficult to find because, hey . . . it's up to you!

ANSWERS TO THE FIND THE DIFFERENCES PUZZLE ON PAGE 122

"p" added
sign changed
door mat added
can missing
telephone different

rolls in shelf added
screw driver added
label added
"ladders" sign different
bill added

123

SNAP-A-PIC

This cartoon trick lets you take a picture of someone
and develop that picture in a second!

Have your subject look directly into the camera lens and smile.
Then, with a quick flip of the page . . . there they are!

HERE'S HOW YOU SNAP-A-PIC!

1. Draw a camera on the lower part of a drawing pad. In the center of the camera, draw a cartoon portrait of a friend (or just draw a zany character to use for anyone). Draw a square around the portrait, then cut through the paper on the top and two sides of the square (see dotted lines).

2. By bearing down hard when you draw the square around the portrait, you will be able to see the imprint of the square on the next page. Draw a sketch of a lens in that box. Then, cut through the bottom and two sides of this square (see dotted lines).

3. Pull the first page back down. Bring the cut out square with the lens on it through to the first page and . . .

4. . . . tuck the cartoon portrait behind that square, as shown here. Now your camera is loaded and ready to *Snap a Pic*! By holding the page at the bottom and quickly lifting it up and down once, it looks as if the lens has miraculously turned into a picture! Try it!

THE DANCIN' MAN!

Here is another cool optical effect.

Hold this page at eye level (like this fella on the left) and quickly blink one eye at a time—right eye, left eye, right eye, left eye, and so on—to see the man dance!

ANSWER TO RIDE 'EM!
(FROM PAGE 123)